ISRAEL: Key to World Peace

Herbert Vander Lugt

Israel: Key to World Peace
Copyright 1981 by
Radio Bible Class
Printed in the United States of America

Contents

1. Israel's History 5
2. Israel's Calling 22
3. Israel's Land 34
4. Israel's Blindness 50
5. Israel's Conversion 72
6. Israel's Glory 87

Introduction

We thank God for periods of tranquillity and freedom, but we have no illusions that man can bring about an era of universal peace and righteousness. A reading of Matthew 24 should convince us that nothing short of the glorious return of Jesus Christ can usher in the golden age of which the Old Testament prophets spoke.

Since this event will not occur until the Jews as a people repent and accept Christ as Savior, we have good reason to say that Israel holds the *key to world peace.* Our Lord, in His last lament over Jerusalem, issued this solemn notice: "I tell you, you will not see Me again until you say, 'Blessed is He who comes in the name of the Lord'" (Matthew 23:29 NIV).

In this book we will discuss and evaluate Israel's past, present, and future relationship with God. We will show how her unbelief, both in history and the current age, has prevented the establishment of God's kingdom upon the earth. We will also see how the Lord will bring about the spiritual rebirth of the Jewish people so that He can fulfill His promises for the coming age of worldwide peace, righteousness, and prosperity.

Herbert Vander Lugt

1. Israel's History

If you were to survey the covers of the well-known weekly news magazines published during the last decade, you would find that they featured many stories about the Middle East. Experts in international affairs look upon this area of the world as a powder keg that could explode into World War III at any moment.

In the heart of this region lies Israel, a tiny nation with a Jewish population of about 3 million people. The strongest military power in that area of the world, it is made up of enterprising, dedicated, and industrious citizens. At great effort and sacrifice, the Israelis have turned arid deserts and murky swamplands into productive fields and farms. They have become world leaders in the production of textiles, are successfully tapping the chemical wealth of the Dead Sea, and have won three wars against numerically superior forces. They look to the future with great hope, convinced that the day is coming when they will be joined by millions of Jews from all over the world to make Palestine the most beautiful and prosperous country on this planet.

Not everyone, however, is sympathetic to the Israelis. The members of the Palestinian Liberation Organization, for example, hate them and insist that Israel has no right to exist as an independent nation. Neighboring Arab countries don't even try to disguise their antagonism. And even those Middle East neighbors who don't take a hostile view are suspicious of every move made by Jewish leaders.

These anti-Jewish feelings are not restricted to the inhabitants of the Middle East. In Russia, Jews are the victims of open discrimination, and most of their requests to emigrate to Israel are denied. Even in the free Western world, Jews are sometimes treated unfairly. They are often caricatured as greedy and dishonest. Militant organizations distribute hate sheets in which they accuse the Jews of instigating all the wars and revolutions of recent history. Some of these extremist writers, taking advantage of the freedom given them in Western democracies, actually portray Hitler as a Christian gentleman who was right in opposing the Jews. They ridicule the claim that 4 to 6 million Jews were slaughtered in Germany, saying that it was a lie invented by the descendants of Abraham to gain world sympathy. These scandal sheets often picture the Jewish community as providing the brains behind the communist conspiracy for world domination. How they dare make this contention in the face of what is happening to Jews in Russia today, nobody knows! But no reputable scholars advocate the views of these radicals, so we need not even dignify their charges with a logical reply.

We should honestly face and answer the basic questions, however, that are being asked today about the Jews. Many people in Bible-believing churches actually know very little about the Jews and the nation Israel. They are completely befuddled when someone makes the outrageous claim that today's Jews are not really Israelis but descendants of the Khazars, a Turkish-language people who lived in the Caucasus during the Middle Ages. They are at a loss to answer pointed questions like: In what way is Abraham the father of the Jews? Can we be sure Israel has a special place in God's program? Do the Jews of our day represent all 12 tribes of Israel or just the two southern tribes?

This chapter, therefore, will present a brief overview of Jewish history from its beginning until the time of Christ. A concise survey should help you see just who the Israelites are and how they came into being as a nation. When God's people understand these basic truths, they will not be misled by militants who make wild and unsubstantiated statements about the Jews.

THE BEGINNING

The origin and earliest history of the Israelites is recorded in Genesis 12-50. God appeared to a man named Abraham, a Chaldean living in the city of Ur, and told him to leave this area where people worshiped the sun god. Abraham obeyed and journeyed to Haran, where he lived until the Lord came to him again with the message that he must move on. He entered Canaan (today's Palestine) at the age of 75 with his family and possessions, and accompanied by his nephew Lot.

Even though the Lord had promised Abraham that his seed would become in number like the stars of the heavens and the sands of the seashore, he and his wife were childless. Sarah apparently concluded that the only way Abraham would have his own son would be through a concubine. In keeping with the common practice of that time, therefore, she gave him her maid Hagar. Through this union Ishmael was born when the patriarch was 86 years old. Abraham undoubtedly believed that this child was the "son of promise," but 13 years later God miraculously rejuvenated him and his wife Sarah, and she gave birth to Isaac.

Many of the peoples of the Middle East trace their lineage back to Abraham. Through his son Ishmael, his children by Keturah, and his grandson Esau, he became the progenitor of numerous kings and nations, including many of the Arabs. But the line of special promise went from Abraham through Isaac to Jacob and his 12 sons.

The closing chapters of Genesis recount the well-known story of Joseph, the eleventh of Jacob's sons. As a young man he was sold into slavery by his brothers but eventually became the prime minister of Egypt. The Lord brought him to this position so that the family of Jacob would leave Palestine to escape a killing drought and move into Goshen, an especially fertile area near the Nile delta. There, under the blessing of God, the Hebrews multiplied rapidly during the next 200 years, free from repeated attacks by the hostile tribes of the Palestine region. Besides, the religious system of Egypt declared the Israelites to be a ceremonially unclean people. This kept the Jews from intermarrying with Egyptians, and adopting their heathen practices, thereby losing their national distinctives.

The nation increased until they numbered more than 2 million people. Undoubtedly they loved the security and prosperity of Goshen. But God decreed that it was time for them to return to Canaan, the land of promise. Therefore He permitted a cruel new dynasty to take over in Egypt. The reigning Pharaoh viewed the Israelites as a threat and took harsh measures to prevent their further growth. He reduced them to slavery and subjected them to unbelievable oppression. Intense suffering bound the Israelites together as a people, reminded them of the living God, caused them to accept the leadership of Moses, and made them willing to leave Goshen.

ERA OF MIRACLES

The next period in the history of Israel can be called an era of miracles. It began with the call of Moses in about 1450 B.C. and ended about 100 years later. The historical narratives of Exodus through Joshua are replete with stories of openly supernatural events. God appeared to Moses in a burning bush, gave him a series of supernatural signs, sent 10 plagues upon the Egyptians, and opened up a path through the Red Sea wide enough to permit the passage of more than 2 million Israelites. God gave His wandering people manna as food, caused water to gush from rocks, kept sandals and clothing from wearing out, and led them on their journey with a pillar of cloud and fire. He spoke audibly to their leaders, opened up the Jordan for their entry into Canaan, flattened the walls of Jericho, and gave them special help in conquering the land. In a period of 16 years under Joshua's leadership, and against superior numbers, they captured most of the land of Palestine.

CONTAMINATION

Though the Israelites had been granted God's supernatural revelation and help, they did not obey Him fully. Even in the time of Joshua they did not obey the Lord's command to rid the land completely of its inhabitants. If those who dwelled in the territory chose to resist the advancing Israelites, they were to be completely annihilated. God gave this order because He didn't want His people contaminated by the wickedness of the Canaanites. True, they had a well-developed culture and advanced farming techniques, but they were immoral beyond description. Even though God wanted them treated as a cancer in the land, Joshua allowed them to remain in some of the fertile valleys. After his death, some of the Israelites married their heathen neighbors, and soon many of them were adopting their vile religious customs.

The period described in the book of Judges lasted about 300 years. Though the Israelites had no central government during that time, anarchy did not prevail because local communities had their own civil rulers. God was worshiped at the tabernacle, a tent located in a place called Shiloh. The worship there and the nationwide observance of Mosaic ordinances were good unifying influences. They were not strong enough, however, to give the people a sense of national unity and to keep them from being contaminated by their heathen neighbors. As a result, a tragic cycle of events began: spiritual conditions in the land would degenerate until the people were far from God. Then the Lord would allow them to be subjugated by a heathen country. In response, the Israelites would repent and cry out for deliverance. God would hear their cry and send a judge to deliver them. But soon the downward cycle would begin again.

The absence of a strong centralized government during the period of the judges had some advantages. It gave the Israelites freedom from heavy taxation and prevented the buildup of a tyrannical bureaucracy. The people benefited from the good rule of some of the local authorities. But because they did not have strong political unity, they were vulnerable to their wicked neighbors—both spiritually and militarily. Therefore, they were unable to carry out the Lord's mandate to conquer the whole land, including the fertile valleys inhabited by the Canaanites.

STRENGTH

Samuel became a priest-judge in Israel shortly after 1100 B.C., and he was an excellent leader. He was greatly loved by the people, and it appears that he gave them a new sense of national unity. But toward the close of his long tenure, the people sent representatives to ask him to give them a king like the other nations. Although he was no doubt offended by this apparent rejection of his leadership, he turned to the Lord for direction. To his surprise, God instructed him to grant their request. But He also told Samuel to warn the people that having a king would mean heavy taxation and the conscription of their sons into hard labor and military service. This didn't dissuade them, however, and soon Saul—a tall, handsome, shy, and humble young man—was crowned as Israel's first king. Though he possessed some fine qualities and led the Israelites to several important victories over old enemies, he did not greatly strengthen the nation. His rule gradually degenerated, and even before his reign had ended the Lord led Samuel to anoint David as the next king of Israel. Shortly after Saul and his sons were killed in battle, David came to the throne.

David was Israel's greatest king. Under his rule, which began about 1000 B.C., the nation became united, strong, and respected. His armies defeated the Philistines so soundly that they never again menaced Israel. He captured Jerusalem and made it the capital of the country. He subdued the surrounding enemy nations that had sought to hinder Israel's growth and made them tributaries. He brought material prosperity to the land and established a fair system of justice. A high cultural climate was encouraged, and music and literature flourished. He brought the ark of the covenant to Jerusalem and had it placed in a special tent. He developed a beautiful system of worship which included the singing of many of his own magnificent psalms.

When David died, his son Solomon ascended the throne. This gifted ruler led the nation in building the temple, a structure of unusual splendor and beauty. He erected many buildings, furthered the development of the arts, and made Jerusalem the envy of the world. His lavish lifestyle and ambitious enterprises, however, placed a great strain upon the people, taxes soared, and many were drafted into labor gangs. Then too, Solomon succumbed to the temptation of marrying foreign women to enhance his position among the kings of the nations, opening the door to paganism. The moral and spiritual trend had turned sharply downward in Israel by the time he died about 930 B.C.

DETERIORATION

Solomon's son Rehoboam was Israel's next king. A proud man, he was warned against continuing the extravagant policies of his father. The people were tired of the heavy taxes, and they didn't want their sons conscripted into government labor. But Rehoboam refused to listen to his wise counselors. Instead, he haughtily informed the people that they could expect even heavier taxes and more forced labor from him than from his father. This was a serious mistake. A gifted young man named Jeroboam led the 10 northern tribes to secede, and he established a separate state. Rehoboam was left with only the tribes of Judah and Benjamin. A little later, the entire tribe of Levi chose to reunite with him, and the two kingdoms went their separate ways. The northern tribes were known as Israel, while the Southern Kingdom was called Judah.

Israel was ruled by several dynasties and never had a good king. From the very outset it began to lose citizens, for many of them emigrated southward to Judah. In 1 Kings 12:23 we are told about a group from the 10 tribes, called "the remnant of the people," who chose to live in the Southern Kingdom.

On two other occasions, large numbers of people left Israel to join Judah. The first took place when King Asa led Judah in a widespread spiritual awakening (2 Chronicles 15:9). The second occurred during the great religious revival under Hezekiah (2 Chronicles 30:25,26). Thus, large numbers of people from the northern tribes were absorbed into the Southern Kingdom.

As the Northern Kingdom continued to degenerate spiritually, it became weaker militarily and industrially. Finally, in 721 B.C., the Assyrians overran the land and deported the most desirable citizens to their own country. They left the lowest working class in their homeland, and many of these people identified themselves with the two southern tribes (2 Chronicles 34:9). The Southern Kingdom, therefore, though beginning with people from only the tribes of Judah and Benjamin, gradually drew into it a significant number of members from all the other tribes.

After Israel's fall, Judah continued to exist as an independent kingdom for another 135 years. The royal family of David remained in power, but most of the kings were not godly men. The few who were, however, led in revivals that temporarily halted the degenerative slide. But the citizens in the Southern Kingdom became increasingly involved in heathen practices and worship, and in 586 B.C. the Babylonians under Nebuchadnezzar captured Jerusalem and subjugated the entire land.

CAPTIVITY

Nebuchadnezzar did the same with Judah that Assyria had done with Israel. He took the most desirable people out of their homeland and planted them in his own colonies. He hoped they would merge with his other subjects, and some of them did. They intermarried with the heathen and were absorbed into the Assyrian, Babylonian, or Persian cultures. Similarly, some of the people who had been left in the area around Jerusalem married heathen mates and became part of the Gentile civilization of that day. But many others, representing all of the tribes (those remaining in Palestine as well as those in various localities throughout the Assyrian, Babylonian, and Persian empires), did not forget their roots. They maintained as much of their national distinctiveness as they possibly could. They remained loyal to Jehovah and the law of Moses, and married their own people. Synagogues were established as instruction centers. They spread out and settled everywhere throughout the ancient world—Asia Minor, Cyprus, Crete, the coastal region of Greece, the islands of the Aegean Sea, Southern Europe, Egypt, North Africa, and even India and China. Everywhere they went they built synagogues for teaching the Mosaic law. They continued to worship Jehovah as their God and considered Jerusalem to be their holy city.

THE RETURN

While many of these representatives from the 12 tribes of Israel were prosperous and happy in their new homes, others longed to return to their native homeland. In 537 B.C., by the authority of the Persian ruler Cyrus, Zerubbabel led a group of Jews back to

Palestine. Some years later, Ezra headed a similar expedition, and they succeeded in rebuilding the city of Jerusalem, reconstructing the walls, and erecting a new temple. These people looked upon themselves as representing the entire 12 tribes. This can be seen clearly in the fact that at the dedication of the temple Ezra offered "twelve he-goats, according to the number of the tribes of Israel" (Ezra 6:17).

In the following years, people from every Jewish tribe continued to trickle back to their homeland. The population increased dramatically in 336 B.C. when Alexander the Great encouraged large numbers of Jews to return to Palestine.

The majority of the Israelites who did not choose to leave the affluence they enjoyed in foreign territories continued to be loyal to the faith of their fathers. Multitudes made pilgrimages to Jerusalem from far and near to celebrate the feasts of the Jewish calendar. Though the inhabitants of Palestine endured a time of terrible persecution shortly after the death of Alexander the Great, they were not destroyed. Nor did they abandon their distinctiveness as God's special people.

At the opening of the New Testament we find that dispersed Jews were still returning to Jerusalem in large numbers to observe the great Hebrew festivals.

This continued until A.D. 70, when Roman soldiers under Titus entered Jerusalem, slaughtered many of its citizens, and completely destroyed the temple and all its adjacent buildings. Then followed a nationwide destruction of Jewish cities and people in A.D. 135, when most surviving Jews were forced to scatter throughout the Roman Empire. From that time until the present century, the Jewish people were dispersed throughout the earth, having no official homeland or center of worship. Through it all, however, they maintained their identity. Then, during the late 1800s and on into the 1900s, gradually larger groups began returning to the land of Palestine. Finally, on May 14, 1948, the independent Jewish state called Israel was established, and a great influx of immigrants came to the struggling new nation.

CONCLUSION

I have presented this historical summary to explain exactly who we have in mind when we talk about the Jews. They are the people who attach themselves to a national heritage which goes back to Abraham and Moses. The vast majority of them are physical descendants of the Israelites of biblical history. Yet this matter of blood descent is not the only element in determining "Jewishness." Some of the members of the 12 tribes married Gentiles and were absorbed into the Persian, Greek, or Roman cultures. Then too, some peoples whose physical ancestry cannot be traced to Abraham have converted to Judaism.

For example, in A.D. 740, the leader of the Turkish-speaking nation called the Khazars accepted the Jewish faith and also led his followers to do so. We cannot be sure how many of their descendants remained loyal to Judaism, but those who did can rightfully be called Jews. They are accepted members of that people for whom God has a special plan. He will someday bring about their national conversion to Christ, restore them to their homeland, and make Jerusalem the world capital. When that happens, all the nations will enjoy a millennium of perfect peace and universal prosperity.

According to the Bible, Israel's history is far from over. In fact, her most glorious days still lie ahead. How important for us, therefore, to keep our eyes upon Palestine, and upon God's chosen people, the Jews!

2. Israel's Calling

Abraham, Isaac, Jacob, Joseph, Moses, Samuel, David, and Daniel are names that are familiar to children who go to Sunday school. These servants of God named in the Old Testament were all Israelites. Other peoples and nations are mentioned, but usually only as they are involved with the Jews.

The New Testament also gives a place of prominence to the Jewish people. When the Lord Jesus sent His apostles on a preaching tour, He told them to go "to the lost sheep of the house of Israel" rather than to Samaritans and Gentiles (Matthew 10:6). And Paul said that the good news he preached as "the power of God unto salvation" was "to the Jew first" (Romans 1:16).

Why does the Bible give such priority to the Jews? What was God's purpose in calling out Abraham and limiting His attention to one line of his descendants? Critics of the Bible charge its writers with narrowminded nationalism, prejudice, and bigotry. They object to the scriptural portrayal of Israel as the chosen nation, saying that God never plays favorites.

But they make these assertions because they ignore or overlook the many passages in the Scriptures that set forth Israel's high calling and task.

In this chapter, therefore, we will look into God's Word to find out the reasons He set apart Abraham, Isaac, and their descendants to be His special people. What was the Lord's purpose? And what is Israel's special calling and task?

SPECIAL REVELATION

The first reason God called out Abraham and his descendants was to make them the receptacle of special revelation. The Lord made a change in His method of self-disclosure when He chose Abraham. Although He had always made Himself known to man, He was now adding a new element to the revealing of Himself and His plan of redemption.

During the centuries from Adam to Abraham, the Lord had revealed Himself and His will to all mankind through what is usually termed *general revelation.* He spoke through the world of nature. He declared moral truths through the voice of conscience. He made known something of His power, wisdom, holiness, and love in His providential ordering and directing of history. In addition, people told each succeeding generation the revealed truths about creation, the fall, and the principle of sacrifice.

The Almighty had expressed these verities clearly to Adam and Eve, and to people like Enoch. But the human race as a whole paid little attention to God. The vast majority worshiped idols and practiced all forms of immorality. By the time of Abraham, only a few people followed the true and living God. But this didn't take Him by surprise. He had planned for this contingency and set in motion with Abraham's call a new program of revelation. Now He would speak directly to a few chosen people and manifest Himself supernaturally to them over a long period of time.

This doesn't mean that God's general revelation stopped with Abraham's call. The apostle Paul declared that pagans could still detect His power and deity through observing the world of nature (Romans 1:19,20). He testified that the heathen continued to "show the work of the law written in their hearts, their conscience also bearing witness, and their thoughts the meanwhile accusing or else excusing one another" (Romans 2:15).

It was only to Abraham, Isaac, Jacob, and the tribes of Israel, however, that He made Himself known as Jehovah, the covenant-keeping God of all mankind. Only in behalf of the Jews did He work mighty miracles of deliverance, such as those in Egypt. No other people was given a pillar of cloud and a pillar of fire as a means of supernatural guidance. No other nation was supernaturally provided with manna from heaven and water from dry boulders. It was only to Israel that the Lord gave the complex and beautiful law-system that was first announced at Mt. Sinai. And only among the Israelites did the Lord inspire men to write a record of His self-revealing words and deeds.

VEHICLE OF WITNESS

Israel's second calling and task was that of being a witness to the nations of the world. He gave Palestine to the Jews as their homeland. This strategic place on earth is located where three continents come closest together. This was the land bridge in the ancient world between the ruling nations. Ezekiel 5:5 tells us that the Lord had set Jerusalem "in the midst of the nations and countries that are round about her." In this passage He was rebuking the people of Israel for setting a terrible example before their neighbors rather than being an effective witness to God's holiness.

To understand Israel's calling and task, we must realize that God never limited His salvation to any one nation. We mentioned earlier that Job and Melchizedek, contemporaries of Abraham, were God-fearing men. This likely indicates that scattered among the heathen were people who truly knew God. Both of these non-Jews understood the principle of blood sacrifice in atonement for sin. The sacrificial aspect of special revelation was therefore still understood by some people outside the chosen line.

Furthermore, even though the Mosaic ritual was given only to Israel, the law-system provided for the inclusion of Gentiles in the blessings of salvation. The "mixed multitude" which left Egypt with the Israelites, as well as the "strangers," could gradually become an integral part of the nation. Clearly, God wanted the Israelites to reach out and bring others into a saving relationship with Himself.

We have no positive indication that the Israelites carried out a systematic program of witness to their neighbors. But their unusual history bore testimony to their faith in the God they served.

Think of what happened in Egypt! Pharaoh and his court saw many miraculous signs performed by Moses, and the entire nation experienced the horrors of the 10 plagues. The people of Canaan had heard reports of God's wonderful works in behalf of His people. We know this because of the story of Rahab. When the Israelites who had entered Jericho as spies came to her home, she let them know that she and her people had heard all about God's miraculous deeds in behalf of His people. (See Joshua 2:9-11.)

God intended Israel's history to be a means of witness. This is clearly declared in the Scriptures. When the Lord gave them His kingdom covenant, for example, in which He made marvelous promises conditioned upon their obedience, He told the Jews that they were to be "a kingdom of priests, and an holy nation" (Exodus 19:6). This statement that they were to be "a kingdom of priests" indicates that just as the priests of Israel mediated between the worshipers and God, so the citizens of Israel were to pass on His blessing to the Gentiles.

We also find evidence of Israel's calling and task in the story of her miraculous crossing of the Jordan River. After the people had walked through the supernaturally opened river, they were commanded to set up 12 stones in Gilgal.

This was to be a memorial for their own descendants, and also "that all the people of the earth might know the hand of the Lord, that it is mighty" (Joshua 4:24).

Israel's extended influence during the prosperous days of David and Solomon carried the message of the living God to all the nations of the Middle East. Sad to say, however, Solomon marred the effectiveness of this witness by marrying heathen women and allowing them to continue their idolatrous practices.

After Solomon died and the nation was split because of the revolt by the northern 10 tribes, spiritual decline continued. Both kingdoms gradually weakened and were attacked by their neighbors. Some of the citizens of these two kingdoms were taken into captivity, and finally both were completely subjugated—Israel by Assyria in 721 B.C. and Judah by Babylon in 586 B.C. Even though the Jews were taken out of their land and into a heathen culture, some of them continued to be a witness for God. In 2 Kings 5 we are told the delightful story about the young Jewish girl who had been taken from her land and made a slave in the home of the Syrian general Naaman.

When she learned that he had leprosy, she boldly told him that he should see the prophet of God. So Naaman got in touch with Elisha, and he was healed. We can be sure that this miracle made a great impact upon many people in the land of Syria.

The story of Daniel and his three friends gives us another example of Israelites bearing witness while in captivity. Their courage even caused King Nebuchadnezzar to make a humble acknowledgment of Israel's God.

During the years of their captivity, the Jewish people were more effective witnesses for Jehovah than ever before. This was partly because they established synagogues wherever they settled. When Cyrus, the Persian ruler, permitted the Jews to return to the land of Palestine, he fulfilled a prophecy expressed by Isaiah and helped the nation of Israel fulfill her calling as a witness. Cyrus had not yet been born when God's spokesman declared,

> I am the Lord, and there is none else, there is no God beside Me; I girded thee, though thou hast not known Me,
>
> That they may know from the rising of the sun, and from the west, that there is none beside Me. I am the Lord, and there is none else (Isaiah 45:5,6).

While captive in Babylon, Israel had been a witness for God. One of the purposes of the remnant's return was that people everywhere might know that the God of Israel is the only true and living

God. The same may be true of Israel's return to Palestine today.

The people who journeyed back to Palestine under Ezra rebuilt the temple and restored the Mosaic ritual. Meanwhile, the Jews still in captivity continued meeting in synagogues, and over the centuries until Christ's death millions of them journeyed to Jerusalem to celebrate the festivals and feast days of the Levitical system.

By New Testament times, many Gentiles had embraced the Jewish faith. Some of them, like the Ethiopian eunuch who was led to Christ by Philip, were *proselytes of righteousness* (Acts 8:26-40). The Roman centurion Cornelius was also a proselyte to the Jewish faith (Acts 10). Those like him were called *proselytes of the gate*. These Gentiles, attracted to the Hebrew concept of one God and linked to Judaism in various ways, were called "devout men." They are described as those "who worshiped God" (see Acts 10:2,7;13:26,43,50;16:40;17:4,17;18:7).

Even though the people of Israel won some converts to their faith while in exile and under Roman rule, they never were really effective in their witness to the nations around them. They did not fulfill God's intended purpose for their existence. They will do so in the millennial age, however, but that is a subject we will be discussing in a later chapter.

CHANNEL FOR THE MESSIAH

The third reason for Israel's call was to provide the physical line through which Messiah would become a member of the human family. The genealogies in the first chapter of Matthew and the third chapter of Luke trace the ancestry of Jesus back from the virgin Mary to David, to Abraham, and to Adam.

When God told Abraham to leave his native country and head for Canaan, He gave this promise: "... in thee shall all families of the earth be blessed" (Genesis 12:3). Later, after the patriarch demonstrated his faith by being willing to offer his son as a sacrifice, the Lord declared, "And in thy seed shall all the nations of the earth be blessed, because thou hast obeyed My voice" (Genesis 22:18). The apostle Paul undoubtedly had this Bible passage in mind when he wrote, "Now to Abraham and his seed were the promises made. He saith not, And to seeds, as of many; but as of one, And to thy seed, which is Christ" (Galatians 3:16). Paul was emphasizing the point that even though this promise was partially fulfilled in the nation of Israel, its ultimate realization was in Jesus Christ.

In Romans 9 the apostle made another reference to Israel's role in providing the channel for our Lord's humanity. After listing the distinctives of this nation—its adoption, glory, covenants, temple service, promises, and fathers—he added "... of whom, as concerning the flesh, Christ came, who is over all, God blessed forever. Amen" (Romans 9:5).

Old Testament history records one attempt after another on the part of Satan to destroy the nation of Israel or the line of David. The enemy was trying desperately to frustrate God's announced purpose for His chosen people, the line through whom the Savior would be born. And at times things did look dark for the nation. The family of David came within a hairsbreadth of extinction. Both the Northern and Southern Kingdoms were taken into captivity. But, unlike many other nations who experienced the same fate, they did not lose their identity. God miraculously preserved both the nation and the line through which the Messiah would come. The Lord's work through Israel was not yet completed. This nation was still to be the human channel for the Messiah and the center of the Kingdom.

CONCLUSION

God called Abraham, Isaac, Jacob, and the tribes of Israel, not only because of His concern for them but also for the spiritual welfare of all mankind. Prior to Abraham's call, the entire human race had departed from Him. Though He had made Himself known to them through nature and conscience, the need for special revelation was obvious.

God called Abraham, his family, and his posterity through Isaac and Jacob, first of all, to be the receptacle of special revelation. He inspired some of their number—historians, poets, prophets—to produce the written Scriptures. He also called upon the nation to be a witness through their history, their unique rituals, and through direct communication of His truth. And He chose the descendants of Abraham through David to become the physical line through which Messiah would become a member of the human race. And in the salvation procured through that divinely sent One, Israel became a blessing to all mankind. Furthermore, as we shall see in future chapters, her role in God's total plan for this world is not yet over.

3.
Israel's Land

The leaders of the United States, Russia, China, England, and other large nations are very much concerned about the Palestine problem. This is primarily because the world's oil supply is closely linked with the relationship between Israel and her neighbors. If a major war were to break out in the Middle East, individual as well as national survival would be threatened. A full-scale military confrontation in Palestine could bring about the destruction of the refineries, storage tanks, pipelines, and ships essential to the production and distribution of oil. Therefore, through diplomatic and other means, both East and West are working for peace.

One explosive issue which must be solved in the Middle East involves the people known as "the Palestinians." The April 14, 1980, issue of *Time* magazine acknowledged this fact, for its cover carried the headline, "The Palestinians: Key to a Mid-East Peace." These people, numbering almost 4 million, are Arabs who insist that they have been forcibly ejected from their homes by the Israelis. More than half a million of them are currently living in squalid, overcrowded camps scattered across the Middle East. They insist that they have a legal right to the land. The Jews, on the other hand, declare that by Divine grant and historical precedent they are entitled to the land of promise.

In this chapter we will study Palestine itself, Israel's land. We will summarize its history, consider its boundaries, and discuss its strategic importance. We will also appraise its geographical and physical characteristics as they relate to God's purpose for calling out the nation of Israel.

THE HISTORY OF THE LAND

The land of Canaan first became important in biblical revelation when God called Abraham to leave his home in Ur of the Chaldeans and move into the area of the earth now known as Palestine. The

Lord gave this territory to the patriarch and his descendants forever. But, as we will see, the Israelites actually occupied it for only a small period of time.

Those wicked Canaanites

The people living in the land of promise when Abraham arrived went by a number of tribal names, but they are all classified as Canaanites. Their ancestry is thought to be closely related to that of the Phoenicians. Even though they developed an advanced culture, they followed an elaborate religious system in which the fertility god Baal held a prominent place. Extreme sexual immorality was an integral part of their worship, and this led them to become unbelievably degraded. In fact, they commonly practiced every perversion known to mankind.

We therefore should not be surprised to learn that after the exodus from Egypt, God commanded the Israelites to show these people no mercy when they invaded the land. The Canaanites had the option of fleeing; but if they chose to stay and fight, they were to be annihilated. The Almighty knew that if the Jews began to associate with these heathen people, they would be contaminated by their evils. But the Israelites did not obey God's order. They allowed the Canaanites to inhabit the valleys and plains in Palestine, and they were a wicked influence upon the Israelites until 1200 B.C. As a result, the 12 tribes adopted many of their heathen practices.

The pesky Philistines

Beginning about 1200 B.C., a new threat to Israel arose—the Philistines. These people apparently drove out or killed most of the Canaanites, thus eliminating that peril. But they became Israel's foes, attacking them repeatedly and keeping them out of the best farming and grazing territories.

The ancestry of the Philistines has never been solidly confirmed. They are often called "sea peoples," and it appears that they came from Crete and the Aegean region. Among their number was a race or family of giants, the remnant of the sons of Anak (Joshua 11:22). If Goliath was a representative member of this group, they were huge indeed, for he was 9 feet 2 inches tall. Their success in controlling large parts of Canaan is clearly indicated by the name still used for this territory, Palestine, which means the "land of the Philistines."

King David finally subjugated the Philistines. But they still retained an area of their own, the section of land between the Mediterranean Sea and the southern tribes.

From the United Monarchy to the Captivity

The entire land of Palestine was brought

under Israel's dominion during the reigns of David and Solomon. The Israelites, however, never did actually occupy all the territory staked out in God's promise to Abraham. But to some extent under David, and more so under Solomon, they did receive tribute from the nations of the Middle East.

This happy situation didn't last long, however. Under Rehoboam, Solomon's son, Israel was divided into two kingdoms. The northern 10 tribes seceded and formed a separate monarchy which went by two principal names—Israel and Ephraim. It was never ruled by a descendant of David. It developed its own pagan religious system, and it soon deteriorated spiritually and economically until its people were taken captive by the Assyrians in 721 B.C.

The tribes of Judah and Benjamin, on the other hand, retained the Davidic dynasty. They experienced a few genuine religious revivals, but they gradually became weak—spiritually, morally, and militarily. In 586 B.C. the Babylonians under Nebuchadnezzar invaded the land and took most of the people as captives. The glory days were over.

Return and Resettlement

The Northern Kingdom ended with the captivity, but many of its citizens united with the people from the two southern tribes. A few of the poorest people remaining in the land merged with other captive people placed there by the Assyrians. The offspring of these marriages formed their own culture, established their own religion, and claimed the area between Judah and Galilee known as Samaria. This was a sizable territory at the time of Christ, but today only a few hundred Samaritans can be found in Palestine.

The territory inhabited by Judah and Benjamin was not repopulated by the Babylonians. The poorer citizens of the Southern Kingdom, left behind, were joined by people from the Northern Kingdom who didn't want to intermarry with Gentiles. Though they grew in number, they remained a rather inconspicuous company of Palestinian citizens. In 538 B.C., after Persia had become the new world power, King Cyrus issued a decree permitting the Jews in his empire to return to Palestine. Many of them responded, and over a period of several years they reconstructed the wall of Jerusalem, built a new temple, and reinstituted the Mosaic system of sacrifices. They were quite independent and secure for almost 200 years.

Alexander, the Ptolemies, the Seleucids

Things changed for the Jews in Palestine about 333 B.C. when they were subdued by Alexander the Great. He probably would have been tolerant of them and their religious practices, but he died suddenly and his kingdom fell into the hands of hostile factions—the Ptolemies (Egyptians) and the Seleucids (Syrians).

The Ptolemies gained control of the Middle East first, and they granted the Jews a great amount of freedom. But in 167 B.C., the Seleucid prince Antiochus Epiphanes came to power. This forceful king was determined to impose his pagan religious practices on the Jews. They revolted under the leadership of a priest named Mattathias and his son Judas. These men, known as the Maccabees, led a guerrilla warfare against the Syrians and succeeded in establishing an independent Jewish state.

Roman Rule

The next nation to exert control over Palestine was Rome. At first they did not oppress the Jews. But when internal dissension among the leaders of Israel threatened the stability of the situation, the Romans intervened. Under General Pompey, armed legionnaires marched into Jerusalem in 63 B.C. They took things firmly into control, but Jewish resentment remained high. Therefore, in 40 B.C., the Romans appointed Herod the Great to be the king of Judea to appease the Jews.

Herod died just a few months after the

birth of Jesus, and this brought another change to the Jews in Palestine. The Romans divided Judea into several tetrarchies, each of which had a Jewish king. But the imperial government insisted upon more control than ever. Once again this produced dissatisfaction among the Jews. Finally they revolted, and Titus brought his efficient armies to lay siege to Jerusalem. He conquered it in A.D. 70, killing most of its inhabitants, completely destroying the temple buildings, and forcing the survivors to disperse. A few years later some of the Jews started filtering back. They mounted another revolt about A.D. 135, but this too ended in disaster. This time the Romans killed hundreds of thousands of Jews and destroyed more than 1,000 villages. They forced them to scatter throughout the then-known world, and the Jews made no serious effort to restore their nation until this present century.

Muslim Domination

Palestine remained under Roman control until the 6th century, when the empire fell. With the rise of Mohammedanism, Palestine gradually became Muslim territory. This infuriated some of the leaders of the Western church. They resented the domination of Islam, viewing it as a desecration of the holy land

and the city over which Jesus had wept. Therefore, they organized seven crusades between A.D. 1096 and 1270 to "liberate" Palestine from Mohammedan control. Though the Crusades have been glamorized by some writers, they were foolish and ill-conceived. Except for one brief period of victory, they were a complete failure. The land of Palestine remained predominantly Muslim with a Christian minority.

Twentieth Century

Today Palestine has once again become the homeland of the Jews. Israel is now a nation of almost 4 million people, and the entire city of Jerusalem is in their hands. The Jews do not occupy any territory east of the Jordan (except for the area northeast of the Sea of Galilee known as the Golan Heights, but they control a large land area. Their presence as a strong military power is a constant source of irritation to the Arab nations, and the Palestinians living in exile complain bitterly that they have been unjustly treated. Israel's leaders deny these charges, and insist that they are seeking a just and equitable solution to the problems of this displaced people.

The presence of Israel back in the land may be seen as a fulfillment of biblical prophecy. The Scriptures foresee a day when the Jews will return to their land and build a new temple. The Bible doesn't tell us whether or not the church will be raptured before that temple becomes a reality. Passages like Daniel 9:27 and 2 Thessalonians 2:4,5 make it clear, however, that the Jews will have a temple when the ruler of the Western World makes a 7-year treaty with them and then breaks it. Reports are circulated from time to time about the Israelis purchasing building materials for their temple, but until now they have been unsubstantiated. Yet the very fact that Israel exists as a nation and that it is an important force in the Middle East must be seen as highly significant. Palestine is the established homeland for the Jewish nation.

BOUNDARIES OF PALESTINE

Israel has a rather sizable area in Palestine today, but it does not possess all the territory God promised to Abraham's descendants through Isaac and Jacob. The Bible teaches that the converted, Christ-honoring Israelis of the future will inhabit a far larger parcel of ground than is occupied today.

We cannot determine with certainty the exact boundaries God had in mind when He promised the land to Abraham. Genesis 15:18 says, " ... from the river of Egypt unto the great river, the river Euphrates." Bible scholars are divided as to whether "the river of Egypt" is the

Nile or the Wadi el Arish, a small stream in the Sinai Peninsula that some maps call "the river of Egypt."

To say that the southern boundary is the Nile presents some serious problems. If it is, that means the Israelites were actually in their own land when they were living in Goshen. And Moses would have been in the Promised Land when he stood at the top of Mount Nebo. But the Israelites knew they were not in the land of promise during the wilderness wandering. And, God had told Moses that He would let him see the Promised Land, but that he couldn't enter it. It seems best, therefore, to view the Wadi el Arish as the southern boundary of Palestine.

The northern extremity of the land promised to Abraham—the river Euphrates—also poses some problems for Bible scholars. As the Euphrates moves northward and westward, it reaches a high point in northern Iraq. This is a tremendously large territory, greatly exceeding the area controlled by David and Solomon. Their empire only touched the lowest point of the Euphrates toward the east. Therefore, the northern boundary of the Promised Land also cannot be established with confidence.

The same difficulty faces us when we seek to determine the eastern extent of the land. We know that the tribes of Gad, Manasseh, and half of Reuben settled to the east of the Jordan. On the basis of Deuteronomy 34:1-4, we can conclude that this was within God's plan. But the territory actually occupied by Israel during the regimes of David and Solomon was not nearly as large as that originally parceled out to the 12 tribes. Moreover, in Ezekiel's prophetic vision of the tribal allotments during the millennium (chapters 40-48), he didn't mention anything east of the Jordan River. Today this land belongs to the country known as Jordan.

It therefore follows that we cannot say exactly what the boundaries of the Promised Land should be. The Scriptures simply do not give us conclusive information. We do know the area from Dan to Beersheba is Israel's, but all other territorial distinctions must be based upon principles of justice and equity.

The boundary problem will not be solved until the Lord Jesus comes as Lord of lords and King of kings and is welcomed by the Jews as their promised Messiah. When He rules as King, He will give Israel all the territory God had in mind in His promise to Abraham.

Interestingly, the dimensions of Palestine throughout Jewish history have been relatively small. The distance from Dan to Beersheba, the northern and southern extremities during Bible days, is only 145 miles. Jerusalem lies only 32 miles inland from the Mediterranean.

The city of Nazareth is only 65 miles from Jerusalem. Thus the great drama of redemption occurred in a postage-stamp-sized area of our globe. But just as God chose the earth, an insignificant planet in a universe containing millions of huge suns, to be the scene of the incarnation, so He has selected this small parcel of land to be the theater of redemption.

STRATEGIC IMPORTANCE

A look at a map shows that Palestine was the crossroads of the ancient civilized world. Because of that, it was a most strategic area.

Palestine was also strategically important because it was located near the center of the fertile crescent. This is a belt of well-watered land in a semi-circular shape that stretches northward from Egypt through Palestine into northern Syria, then curves down through the Mesopotamian plain all the way to the Persian Gulf. The lands in the north were made fertile by irrigation from the Euphrates. In Egypt, the water came from the Nile. The area between the northern and southern extremities were made excellent agricultural land as a result of abundant rainfall.

Located between great civilizations to the north and south, and bounded by the Mediterranean on one side and rugged mountains on the other, Palestine offered the only natural trade route available. Thus Israel was beautifully situated to fulfill her calling to be a witness of God's grace to the entire world.

PHYSICAL CHARACTERISTICS

Palestine is a land of mountains and valleys, not of rolling plains. The tiny Jordan River is nothing like the Nile or Euphrates. The soil of Palestine is reddish in color, indicating a lack of organic matter. Though rich in iron and alkalines, it doesn't grow crops like the deep topsoil of a state like Iowa. But when God told Moses that He would bring Israel out of Egypt, He described Canaan as a "large and good land, ... a land flowing with milk and honey" (Exodus 3:8). A short time later, when Israel sent spies to see what Canaan was like, they came back with pomegranates, figs, and a cluster of grapes so large it had to be carried on a pole between two men. And just before his death, Moses spoke of the blessedness the Israelites would experience when they entered their "land of grain and wine" (Deuteronomy 33:28).

The actual conditions of the land in many ways seem to contradict the oft-repeated description of it as "flowing with milk and honey." The hilly terrain, the reddish soil, and the years of neglect before 1948 give the impression that Palestine is a difficult place to farm.

What about this apparent contradiction between reality and the biblical portrayal of the land? First of all, the land was not barren and bleak when the Israelites first entered it. Its hills were clothed with forests. The low marshy lands were covered with verdant grasses. But when trees are cut down indiscriminately, goats and sheep are allowed to overgraze, and erosion washes away good topsoil, a rich territory soon becomes scrubby and barren. The Israelis today are reclaiming the land by planting many trees, irrigating, and fertilizing the soil. Many blighted areas have already been transformed into productive fields and fruitful vineyards. But much still remains to be done.

At first we may wonder why God would give His people a country with hilly terrain. But when we reflect a little, we can see that He did so for a very specific purpose. At that time, trees and vegetation kept erosion under control, and the topsoil had not yet been washed away. In those conditions people could do very well if they worked hard and planned intelligently. The land was not suited to the lazy, careless, or shortsighted. The water of the heavy winter rainfall had to be conserved. The trees on hillsides had to be harvested carefully, and new ones had to be planted to keep the soil from eroding. The fields had to be protected from overgrazing, or the grass would be replaced by bare soil or worthless scrub. The very characteristics of the land of Palestine, therefore, encourage—even demand—the virtues of industry and foresight. This is another indication that God had a good reason to choose this area of earth as the homeland for His people.

CONCLUSION

Though Israel continues to reject Christ, the time is coming when the Promised Land will be the scene of many stupendous happenings. Ezekiel 38 and 39 describe the supernatural destruction of Russia's armies as they come down from the north to invade the land of Palestine. Daniel 11:36-45 and Zechariah 14:1-8 tell us about the war of Armageddon to be fought in the Valley of Megiddo near Jerusalem. And a number of other Old Testament prophecies depict the time when Jesus Christ will return in power and glory to restore His ancient people, make Jerusalem earth's capital city, and rule over all mankind with justice. Truly, the key to world peace lies with the nation called Israel and the land known as Palestine.

4.
Israel's Blindness

Whether the world in general is sympathetic to the Jews or not, it certainly has to admire them. Without a homeland, they have maintained their national and cultural distinctives for nearly 2 millenniums. Since their return to Palestine in 1948, they have accomplished wonders in that formerly unproductive land. Down through the centuries, they have given the world some of its most out standing leaders. Their people have made great contributions in music, literature, science, and economics. And everyone acknowledges with admiration their devotion to their way of life and their determination to survive under the most adverse and difficult circumstances.

In spite of these accomplishments, however, the Jews have walked in spiritual blindness. In Old Testament days they worshiped pagan idols. They rejected and crucified their Messiah. And the apostle Paul indicated that only a small percentage of them, a "remnant according to the election of grace," would turn to Christ during the church age. He pointed out that "the rest were blinded" (Romans 11:5,7).

During the ministry of Jesus Christ in Palestine, the Jewish people rejected His teaching and were determined to kill Him. He therefore warned them that they were in danger of being plunged into spiritual darkness, saying,

> Walk while ye have the light, lest darkness come upon you...
>
> While ye have light, believe in the light, that ye may be the sons of light (John 12:35,36).

But the Jews wouldn't listen. Not to Him. Not to the apostles. Not to the witness of Christians throughout the last 1,900 years. For that reason, I believe, the world has been plagued by revolutions and wars throughout this entire era. The Bible makes it clear that the Lord Jesus will not come back to establish His kingdom until Israel as a nation repents and turns to Him.

The apostle Peter, while preaching to the Jews shortly after our Lord's ascension to Heaven, stated specifically that Jewish repentance was a prerequisite to the return of the Prince of Peace. He pleaded with his countrymen,

> Repent, then, and turn to God, so that your sins may be wiped out, that times of refreshing may come from the Lord, and that He may send the Christ, who has been appointed for you—even Jesus (Acts 3:19 NIV).

The "times of refreshing" mentioned here is a reference to the millennial age of Revelation 20. The Old Testament prophets pictured that golden era as being initiated by the appearance of Israel's Messiah.

God called out the Israelites to be His special people, and promised that He would bring spiritual and material blessings to all mankind through them. But from the very beginning, the unbelief and sin of the Jews has stood in the way of their fulfilling this role. In this chapter, therefore, I will present a brief historical summary of Israel's failure to trust God and obey His commandments. I will also analyze her sin and unbelief, and then show how God's grace will triumph in the end.

THE WILDERNESS SOJOURN

The family of Jacob grew to the size of a nation while in Egypt. But the independent national existence of the Jews did not begin until after their release from Egyptian bondage, while they were in the wilderness. During the exodus, God made a special covenant with the nation of Israel and gave them a beautiful civil and ceremonial system called the Mosaic law.

The Jews were certainly a privileged people. God delivered them from Egypt through a series of miracles. He opened the Red Sea for them so that they could march across it on dry ground. He provided manna in the wilderness. He kept their clothes from growing old and their shoes from wearing out. He delivered them from their enemies.

But somehow the people seemed ungrateful. As soon as they encountered problems, they complained bitterly against Moses and the Lord. Whenever they faced a water, food, or military crisis, they openly expressed their wish that they had remained in Egypt. And less than 40 days after they unitedly declared, "All that the Lord hath spoken we will do" (Exodus 19:8), they made and worshiped a golden calf, an idol similar to those revered by the wicked Canaanites. And less than 18 months after they had left Egypt, as they stood at the borders of Palestine, they decided that they would prefer to return to Egypt than to march into the land of Canaan (see Numbers 13,14). These Israelites simply were not willing to trust God for the victory He had promised them over the inhabitants of the land!

This act of unbelief profoundly displeased God, so He pronounced a severe judgment upon them. He sentenced them to 40 years of wandering in the wilderness. He further declared that every Israelite 20 years and older would die in this desert area—everyone except Caleb and Joshua, the only men who had demonstrated their faith by urging the people to enter Canaan.

During the period of almost 40 years that followed, an average of 85 Israelites died every day—a vivid reminder of God's displeasure with their unbelief. The seriousness of this sin is also expressed in the New Testament, "But with whom was He grieved 40 years? Was it not with them that had sinned, whose carcasses fell in the wilderness?" (Hebrews 3:17).

Even so, the Lord spoke of the wilderness wanderings as Israel's infancy stage of her history—a time when He loved her very much. In Hosea we read, "When Israel was a child, then I loved him, and called My son out of Egypt" (Hosea 11:1). Though this verse is quoted in Matthew 2:15 as pointing to our Lord's early childhood in Egypt, it is primarily a statement about the nation of Israel. Apparently

God looked upon the murmuring and disobedience in the wilderness as indications of immaturity, not as deliberate rebellion. A baby howls in protest against the loving care of his parents because he does not understand what they are doing. The Israelites, during the infant stage of their national existence, murmured and complained and sinned, evidently without realizing fully what they were doing.

The magnitude of Israel's sin in the wilderness is also somewhat played down by Jeremiah, for he portrayed that nation as the newly wedded wife of Jehovah (see Jeremiah 2:2,3).

The "marriage ceremony" between Jehovah and the young nation took place at Mount Sinai. God's proposal was, "... if ye will obey My voice indeed, and keep My covenant, then ye shall be a peculiar treasure unto Me above all people" (Exodus 19:5). And the Israelites answered, "All that the Lord hath spoken we will do."

Though these very same people sinned almost immediately afterward, they conducted themselves as a submissive bride during the remaining 38 1/2 years of their wilderness sojourn. They built the tabernacle according to God's specifications. Even those who knew that they would die before entering Canaan walked with the Lord in obedience because they recognized His concern for them.

JOSHUA AND THE JUDGES

During the 400 or so years covered by the books of Joshua and Judges, the Israelites were guilty of two sins: (1) incomplete obedience and (2) religious compromise. But they never fully departed from the Lord, and they quickly returned to Him in repentance whenever He disciplined them.

The sin of incomplete obedience occurred when the Israelites marched into Canaan under the leadership of Joshua. With supernatural help from God the Jews swept through Palestine, capturing every fortified city. This made them secure against enemy attack. But some of the Canaanites fled into the valleys, and the Israelites did not pursue and destroy them. This was in direct disobedience to God's explicit orders to drive out or slay every inhabitant of the land. By letting these morally degraded people live next to them, the Jews made themselves vulnerable to their evil influence.

The Israelites began to reap the harvest of this sin soon after Joshua died. Because the Canaanites inhabited the valleys and plains, it became profitable for the Israelites to have business dealings with them. These natives of Canaan, though terribly immoral as a result of practices associated with their worship of the fertility gods, had an advanced civilization. They could teach the Israelites about farming, mining, and manufacturing. No wonder the Canaanites influenced the Lord's people!

It wasn't long before the Israelites began to adopt some of the heathen practices of their neighbors, combining them with elements of their own worship of Jehovah. This was their second sin—religious compromise. It greatly displeased the Lord, for He had warned them at Sinai that He is a "jealous God" (Exodus 20:5). So, He chastened the Israelites. They experienced crop failures, enemy attacks, and periods of servitude to neighboring nations. But whenever these calamities would come, the Israelites were quick to repent of their sin and plead with God for deliverance. In each instance He responded by raising up a judge to lead them in victory over their oppressors. This cycle of events was repeated 12 times during the period covered by the book of Judges.

Even though the Israelites sinned by incomplete obedience under Joshua, and by religious compromise during the period of the Judges, they never repudiated Jehovah. The one was a logical outgrowth of the other. If they had destroyed all the Canaanites as God commanded, they would not have learned about their religious practices.

In spite of the cycle of sinning, judgment, rescue, and repentance, the Jews maintained their allegience to the one true God. The book of Ruth gives us an accurate picture of true piety among many of the Lord's people during this period of their history.

THE MONARCHIAL PERIOD

The nation of Israel reached both its highest and lowest spiritual points while under the rule of the kings. The monarchy began with Saul in 1050 B.C. and ended with Zedekiah in 586 B.C.

The thirteen tribes (counting Levi) were united during the reigns of Saul, David, and Solomon. Although Saul committed a number of personal blunders and sins, even going to a witch for advice on the night before his death, he was loyal to God. And he had some success in his efforts to eliminate idolatry from the land.

The nation reached its highest spiritual plateau, however, under David. He made Jerusalem the center of a beautiful and praise-filled system of worship. And the people sang many of his lofty psalms in praise of Jehovah.

Solomon continued in his father's footsteps during the first part of his rule and led the nation in building the temple for the Lord. This was one of the most magnificent buildings of the ancient world. He also promoted music and singing in the praise of God. But Solomon wanting to emulate other oriental kings, took to himself many wives from various countries. And to please them, he let them worship their pagan deities on altars he himself provided, thus introducing elements of heathenism into Jerusalem itself. This led to spiritual deterioration, which gained momentum after he died.

After Solomon's death, 10 northern tribes seceded from the united kingdom to form an independent nation. They soon fell deeply into religious apostasy. Jeroboam, the new nation's first king, didn't want his people to worship in Jerusalem, so he established religious centers at Dan in the far north and Bethel in the south. He erected golden images of calves that were to be vehicles for the worship of Jehovah. But his claim of loyalty to Israel's God was nothing but a subterfuge. The people plunged rapidly into wicked idolatry.

God sent Elijah and Elisha to the people of the Northern Kingdom with the message of repentance. He gave these prophets miracles and signs as tokens that they were truly from Him. Through their leadership many Israelites abandoned idolatry and began to worship the Lord. But the vast majority of the people paid no attention to these outstanding prophets. Nor would they listen to men like Jonah, Amos, and Hosea. The northern tribes did not experience a single spiritual revival throughout their history, and again God's chastening became inevitable. Assyria finally invaded their land in 721 B.C. and took most of the people into captivity.

Though the southern two tribes did not deteriorate morally and spiritually as quickly as their northern neighbors, there was a gradual decline. They had the advantage of the Davidic dynasty, which gave them eight good kings. Then too, the temple city of Jerusalem was within their geographical territory, serving as a focal point of allegiance to God.

Rehoboam, whose blunder had led to the secession of the northern 10 tribes, was the first to lead the nation away from God. He had altars built in high places and equipped them with images that honored the Canaanite god Baal, and Ashtoreth, his female counterpart. Judah's first king also allowed male prostitutes to be part of the ritual of these sanctuaries and shrines. What a terrible beginning for the newly formed Southern Kingdom!

During the remaining years of Judah's history, 10 of the kings who ruled "did evil in the sight of the Lord." The eight godly kings tried to bring about a return to Jehovah. Though they led the nation in genuine spiritual revivals, they never succeeded in completely uprooting the heathen practices from the land.

God also sent great prophets to Judah—men like Micah, Isaiah, Nahum, Jeremiah, Zephaniah, and Habakkuk. But most of the people refused to heed their warnings and pleas. The populace gradually became more and more entangled in idolatry, and the nation grew increasingly wicked. Finally, in 586 B.C., the Babylonians invaded Jerusalem and took the best citizens of Judah into captivity.

The sins of both kingdoms during the years of their brief independent histories were deeper and more reprehensible than those of their ancestors. Their behavior was even more wicked than that which occurred in the wilderness and during the time recorded in the books of Joshua and Judges. Beginning with their very first rulers, Jeroboam and Rehoboam, they willfully and wantonly turned away from God to the worship of idols because they enjoyed the immoral practices associated with it. And they wouldn't listen to God when He spoke to them through judgments and the prophets. Stephen, the first martyr of the Christian church, summed up the wickedness of both kingdoms when he said to His Jewish persecutors,

> Ye stiff-necked and uncircumcised in heart and ears, ye do always resist the Holy Spirit; as your fathers did, so do ye.
>
> Which of the prophets have not your fathers persecuted? And they have slain them who showed before of the coming of the Just One (Acts 7:51-52).

CAPTIVITY AND DISPERSION

The captivities had a generally good spiritual and moral impact upon the people of both Israel and Judah. In the exile, people from all the tribes banded together in the small communities they were taken to. Members of the Northern Kingdom, acknowledging that their religious heritage went back to Moses and David, gradually merged with the people of Judah, Benjamin, and Levi. All were determined to maintain their cultural and religious distinctives. They organized into congregations governed by elders, and they met in buildings called synagogues. Each of these became the local Jewish center of worship, education, and civil government.

Living in exile and coming into direct contact with heathenism seems to have cured the Jews of idolatry. It strengthened their resolve to worship the one true God revealed in their Scriptures.

Nevertheless, the Israelites were influenced in other ways by their new environment. Some of their scholars incorporated elements of Greek thought into their religious system. Other men reacted to these compromises by becoming extremely legalistic, which laid the foundation for the rise of a strict sect known as the Pharisees. We learn from the gospels and Acts that members of this influential religious group were among the most determined opponents of Jesus Christ and His apostles.

Overall, developments during the intertestamental period were encouraging. A renewed emphasis was given to personal religion, including a deep consciousness of sin and a keen desire for godliness. Moreover, some of the Jews became zealous propagandists and missionaries for their faith, and made a strong appeal to the thinking segment of the pagan world. The Gentiles were attracted to Judaism because of its high ethical content and monotheism, and thousands of them became proselytes to the religion of the Old Testament. These converts became known among the Jews as "God-fearers."

Contact with Grecian culture, combined with proselyting zeal, gave rise to the preparation and distribution of the

Septuagint, a Greek translation of the Hebrew Scriptures. During this same time the Targums came into existence. These were Aramaic paraphrases or interpretive translations of sections of the Hebrew Old Testament.

In general, the Jews in exile were granted a lot of liberty. This helped them economically as well as religiously, and many of them settled down and established successful businesses. They had the money to build synagogues and to hire teachers for their children. As a result, when the opportunity came to return to Palestine, the majority preferred to stay where they were. But they were glad for all who did return, and they were willing to contribute generously for the rebuilding of Jerusalem and the temple. Through their synagogues they maintained their natural and cultural distinctiveness. Many traveled to Jerusalem periodically to celebrate the feasts of Israel. At the beginning of the Christian era, an estimated 3 to 5 million Jews lived outside Palestine. They were known as "the diaspora," the "scattered ones" of Israel.

As we evaluate the spiritual condition of the Jewish people living outside of Palestine during the interval between 600 B.C. and the time of Christ, we observe both good and bad elements. Favorable were these factors: (1) A disdain for polytheism and idolatry. (2) The building of synagogues as centers for retaining religious and cultural distinctives. (3) An emphasis in the home upon the sacredness of marriage. (4) A recognition of the need for a personal walk with God. (5) A zeal to communicate the knowledge of Jehovah to their heathen neighbors.

The main negative feature was a growing tendency toward legalism by the religious leaders. They reinterpreted the Mosaic ordinances, turning them into a merit system for earning favor with God—not a schoolmaster to grace as intended. By the time of Christ, this complete misunderstanding of the Mosaic law was deeply ingrained in Jewish thinking. As a result, when the message of salvation through faith alone was proclaimed, it became a stumblingblock for multitudes of Jewish people.

FROM CHRIST TO TODAY

The religious history of the Jews throughout the entire New Testament era and church age can be summarized by one word: unbelief. This took place in three stages. (1) The Jews rejected Christ and played the major role in His crucifixion. (2) They bitterly opposed the preaching of the apostles. (3) They have continued to resist the witness of Christians for 1,900 years.

The Rejection of Christ

The Jewish religious leaders hated Jesus Christ from the very beginning of His ministry. They were especially incensed by His claim to be the eternal Son of God. They were angered whenever He attacked their hypocrisy and legalism. All in all, they saw Him as a powerful threat to their religious system. By a concerted effort they finally succeeded in bringing about His death by crucifixion.

Perhaps the majority of the Jews in the first century would have believed on Jesus Christ had it not been for the influence of their leaders. The people yearned for political independence, and they responded enthusiastically when John the Baptist came proclaiming the message, "Repent; for the kingdom of heaven is at hand" (Matthew 3:2). When Jesus initiated His ministry with the same proclamation, thousands of Jewish people enthusiastically followed Him. They were thrilled when they saw His miracles, and they recognized that His teaching had the ring of authority. But when it gradually became clear that this Jesus was not about to lead a revolt against the Roman government, many of the Jews were disenchanted. They wanted a political deliverer—not a Messiah like Jesus, who made high ethical and moral demands for personal sacrifice and holiness.

The sin of the Jews in rejecting Christ may have been somewhat mitigated by the fact that they didn't fully understand Him—either His person or His ministry. Their comprehension of the Old Testament Scriptures had no room for a meek, suffering, dying, resurrected Messiah. This concept to them was inconceivable, for they were looking for a strong leader who could free them from Roman oppression. That is why the apostle Peter, addressing a Jerusalem crowd shortly after our Lord's death, could say, "And now, brethren, I know that through ignorance ye did it, as did also your rulers" (Acts 3:17). We can be sure that most of the Jewish people who called for Christ's execution, shouting, "His blood be on us and our children," didn't realize what they were saying.

We must also recognize, however, that an element of willful and deliberate unbelief was involved on the part of many of the Jewish leaders. This is evidenced in the encounter between the Pharisees and Christ recorded in Matthew 12:24-32. When they accused Jesus of performing His miracles by the power of Beelzebub, the prince of the demons, they knew they were speaking falsely. It was a deliberate rejection of truth when they ascribed to the forces of evil that which was obviously being done through the power of the Holy Spirit.

The Apostolic Message

The first apostles were all Jews. They witnessed fervently to their own countrymen of their personal encounters with the risen Christ. They zealously proclaimed Him as the Messiah who fulfilled Old Testament prophecy. But the Jews as a nation still rejected Jesus of Nazareth.

True, quite a number of individual Israelites came to know the Lord Jesus as their Savior. But the religious and political representatives of the people continued to oppose the gospel with bitter intensity. They had the apostles thrown into prison (Acts 5:17-28). They had them beaten with rods (Acts 5:40). They sentenced Stephen to death by stoning (Acts 7). Zealous Pharisees like Saul of Tarsus rounded up Christians for imprisonment, flogging, even execution.

The unbelief of these Jewish leaders during the apostolic age was inexcusable. It could *not* justifiably be said of them, as Peter had said of Christ's persecutors, "I know that through ignorance ye did it" (Acts 3:17). They knew full well that Jesus Christ had been resurrected from the grave. They had firsthand encounters with witnesses who had seen the risen Lord and had talked with Him. They had bribed the guards stationed at the tomb of Jesus, instructing them to circulate the story that the disciples had stolen the body. They even saw the marvelous transformation in the lives of the apostles. In spite of all this evidence, they stubbornly refused to believe. Their resistance continued even when the apostle Peter assured them that if they would repent, their sins would be blotted out, and that God would send Jesus back to bring in the "times of refreshing" prophesied in their Scriptures (see Acts 3:19-23).

The Present Unbelief

The vast majority of the Jewish people are still living in unbelief. Except for a small percentage who have accepted the Lord Jesus as Savior, they wander in a religious "no man's land." Even the zealous Israelis living in Palestine today cannot follow the teachings of Moses to the letter, because the Jews have no temple. Besides, few of them would if they could. Three million Jews are back in Palestine, but they have no unified, life-transforming, satisfying system of religious belief.

Hosea was describing their present state when he wrote, "For the Israelites will live many days without king or prince, without sacrifice or sacred stones, without ephod or idol" (Hosea 3:4 NIV). No descendant of David rules today as the king or prince of Israel. They have no temple, and therefore no sacrificial system. Nor do they possess the sacred stone associated with the Urim and Thummim by which the high priest (dressed in his sacred ephod) could discern the will of God. To their credit, however, they no longer worship idols. Nor do they consult lying teraphim as they did when they had kings.

Amazingly, the Israelites have remained a distinct entity on the earth. They have succeeded in spite of impossible circumstances, severe persecution, and fierce hatred. Eric Sauer made the following comment:

> No people is so capable as the Jew of keeping separate yet being so widespread. No other is so national and yet at the same time so universal. No other preserves so tenaciously its individuality and also remains in the midst of other peoples so self-contained and secluded. Yet again, no other so understands how to attach himself to all places and accommodate himself to all circumstances as does the Jew. The Jew settles down in all places, is able to make room for himself everywhere, and yet everywhere remains a Jew! (*The Dawn of World Redemption,* Eerdmans, Grand Rapids, Michigan, 1952, pp. 110,111).

CONCLUSION

We have traced the sin and unbelief of the Jewish people from the beginning of their history until the present moment. We have discussed some of their positive spiritual accomplishments, and noted their marvelous suitability for the task of being God's special people. Yet, in spite of all their failures, they remain distinct. And God has a special program for them that will culminate in worldwide blessing.

The Bible teaches that the Israelites hold the key to worldwide peace. When they repent and accept Jesus of Nazareth as their Messiah, they will open the door of God's richest blessings for all mankind. The prophet Hosea, after describing the nation's present state, made this marvelous prediction:

> Afterward the Israelites will return and seek the Lord their God and David their king. They will come trembling to the Lord and to His blessings in the last days
> (Hosea 3:5 NIV).

5. Israel's Conversion

In a gripping passage, the prophet Jeremiah described a group of people enduring such intense suffering that every face was pale with torment. Then he cried,

> Alas! for that day is great, so that none is like it; it is even *the time of Jacob's trouble,* but he shall be saved out of it (Jeremiah 30:7).

As Daniel was about to conclude his prophecy, he predicted a similar scene:

> And at that time shall Michael stand up, the great prince who standeth for the children of thy people, and there shall be *a time of trouble,* such as never was since there was a nation even to that same time; and at that time thy people shall be delivered,

everyone that shall be found written in the book (Daniel 12:1).

The Lord Jesus, describing the period just before His glorious return, made this solemn pronouncement:

> For then shall be *great tribulation,* such as was not since the beginning of the world to this time, no, nor ever shall be.
>
> And except those days should be shortened, there should no flesh be saved; but for the elect's sake those days shall be shortened (Matthew 24:21,22).

Each of these Scriptures speaks of a time of unprecedented distress for all mankind, but especially for the Jews. Yet they also promise deliverance for some. The time reference is the great tribulation. This 7-year period of the outpouring of God's wrath, involving every nation, will focus upon Israel. Furthermore, this "time of Jacob's trouble" is a direct prerequisite to the coming of world peace.

In this chapter we will investigate six elements of the great tribulation that have a unique bearing upon God's ancient people. As we do, we will indicate how this dreadful era is designed to bring about the conversion of the Jews as a nation. When this occurs, they will finally fulfill their destiny, and peace will come to our troubled world.

AN ASSURING TREATY

Sometime in the future, perhaps very soon, the Israelis will agree to a 7-year pact with a prominent political leader in the Western World. We don't know if this man will be the head of one major power or of a confederacy of nations when the treaty is signed; but whichever the case, he will have enough clout to give Israel a sense of security.

This treaty is prophesied in Daniel 9:24-27, where the prophet refers to God's program for Israel as covering "seventy weeks." Since the Hebrew word translated "weeks" means "sevens," the reference is obviously to sevens of years. The seventy weeks therefore equals 490 years.

When Daniel gave his prophecy, this time period of 490 years was entirely in the future. The era began during the fifth century before Christ was born, when Israel returned from exile in Babylon. Some scholars say it started with the decree allowing Ezra to lead a return in 458 B.C. Taking the 69 weeks as 483 chronological years, they conclude that the period ended in A.D. 26, the time our Lord began His public ministry. Other Bible teachers reckon the time from 444 B.C., a similar decree mentioned in Nehemiah 2. Using 360-day prophetic years as their standard of measurement, they arrive at A.D. 31, the year of our Lord's crucifixion, as the date Daniel had in mind when he spoke of Messiah being "cut off" (v. 26).

Our concern for this study, however, is in the fulfillment of the remaining week of the 70 weeks, an era yet to come. We also need to identify the other prince mentioned by Daniel, the ruler who will make the 7-year treaty with Israel. A wicked, God-hating man, he will become the head of a Western confederacy of nations, the revived Roman Empire. It will stretch from the Middle East through Western Europe, perhaps including the United States. When the treaty is made, Israel will feel secure.

AN AMAZING DELIVERANCE

A second element closely associated with the great tribulation will be Israel's supernatural deliverance from an invasion by a powerful Northern confederation (see Ezekiel 38 and 39). Enough data is given for us to identify the nation heading this military operation and show how it fits into the endtime picture.

The country leading this onslaught from the north will be Russia. The opening words of Ezekiel 38 make this identification quite positive for several reasons: (1) The land is named *Magog*. Josephus tells us that the Magogites were known by the Greeks as Scythians, a people who settled along the Caucasus Mountains and the Caspian Sea. (2) "Meshech" and "Tubal" are probably ancient tribal names for Moscow and Tobolsk, prominent Russian cities. (3) The Hebrew word rendered as the adjective "chief" by the King James translators is *rosh* (38:2). But it may also be a proper noun. If so, many authorities agree that the inhabitants of Scythia, from whom the modern Russians derived their name, were once called the *rhos* or *rosh* peoples. (4) The single great world power located directly north of Israel is Russia.

The time when this attack will occur is indicated by two expressions, "in the latter years" and "they shall dwell safely, all of them" (Ezekiel 38:8). The invasion will come when Israel feels most secure. This condition will no doubt prevail when the Jews in Palestine have received the assurance of protection by the Western World leader identified in Daniel 9:27. It appears very likely that Russia and her confederates will launch the attack shortly before the midpoint of this 7-year agreement.

Though the armies of Russia will march boldly into the mountains of Palestine, they will never actually do battle with the forces of Israel and her allies. God Himself will intervene, pouring out His wrath upon the invading armies and using supernatural means to destroy them (Ezekiel 38:18-22). This awesome display of His power will make a profound impact upon the world. Multitudes of Jews and Gentiles will acknowledge Him, and many will turn to Him through faith in Christ. (See Ezekiel 39:7.)

A VICIOUS BETRAYAL

A third element closely related to the great tribulation is the vicious betrayal of the Jewish people by the Western ruler with whom they made their treaty. According to Daniel's prophecy, he will suddenly turn against them.

> He will confirm a covenant with many for one "seven," but in the middle of that "seven" he will put an end to sacrifice and offering. And one who causes desolation will place abominations on a wing of the temple until the end that is decreed is poured out on him (Daniel 9:27 NIV).

The Jews will either have their new temple when this political ruler makes his covenant with them, or they will begin construction as soon as the ink is dry. A system of sacrifice and worship will be instituted. But the man in whom they have put such trust will suddenly turn against them. He will place an image of himself in their temple, demand that they worship it, and bitterly persecute all who refuse (read Daniel 9:27; Matthew 24:15; 2 Thessalonians 2:3,4; and Revelation 13).

The people who resist him will be Christians, men and women who have turned to Christ at some time after the rapture of the church. Many will be martyred for their faith. The apostle John, who gave us so many details concerning the great tribulation in Revelation, spoke of a great unnumbered throng of martyred inhabitants of Heaven. He said they will be from "every nation, tribe, people and language"(NIV), and added, "These are they who came out of the great tribulation, and have washed their robes, and made them white in the blood of the Lamb" (Revelation 7:14). Since every nation and tribe on earth is represented in this company, we can be sure it includes Jews and Gentiles from all over the world. Apparently the great tribulation, this most terrible time in all human history, will produce a great harvest of redeemed people who have trusted in Jesus Christ for their personal salvation.

When the persecution by Antichrist begins, large numbers of Jews will scatter throughout the world in an attempt to escape his wrath. They will witness of their faith in Christ, and multitudes will accept Him. Non-believers, Jew and Gentile alike, will comply with the evil ruler's demands, but those who have turned to the Savior will resist. Some of the Jewish people will be supernaturally protected from harm (Revelation 12:13-17), but Zechariah stated that two-thirds of the Jews living in Palestine will be killed during the great tribulation (Zechariah 13:8,9). The treacherous breaking of the treaty will bring untold hardship upon the Jewish people as a whole, but it will also lead to the conversion of many among them.

A MIRACLE TIME

Still another element associated with the great tribulation will be an array of supernatural signs. Some of them will occur in the natural world. Awesome and frightening sights, both in the sky and upon the earth, will appear in abundance. Jesus spoke of them as follows:

> And there shall be signs in the sun, and in the moon, and in the stars; and upon the earth distress of nations, with perplexity; the sea and the waves roaring;
>
> Men's hearts failing them for fear, and for looking after those things which are coming on the earth; for the powers of heaven shall be shaken (Luke 21:25,26).

Revelation 8 tells of four angels sounding trumpets of judgment, one after the other. As they do, cataclysmic disturbances will take place upon the earth and in the sky. The world will be shaken by terrible disasters, bringing suffering and death to millions.

Some people will be given the power to work miracles. The two witnesses depicted in Revelation 11:3-14 will perform amazing supernatural feats. When they have "finished" their testimony, they will be slain, and their dead bodies will be put on public display for 3 1/2 days. After this, to the amazement of all mankind, God will suddenly cause them to stand upon their feet, and then take them up to Heaven.

By the same token, evil men, including the first and second "beasts" of Revelation 13, will also perform miracles, and multitudes will be deceived.

The great tribulation will therefore be a time of wonders reminiscent of the apostolic era. Both followers of God and representatives of Satan will produce amazing demonstrations of the supernatural. This will force people to choose between two options: the devil's way or God's. The people who decide for the Lord will be dreadfully persecuted and many will die. Those who worship the beast and his image will not be persecuted, but they will find little peace and satisfaction in life. Terrible judgments will fall upon them, and they will be judged and slain when Christ returns.

A DRAMATIC APPEARANCE

The great tribulation will culminate in the dramatic appearance of Jesus Christ. This event is graphically portrayed in numerous passages of Scripture.

Zechariah 14, for example, pictures Jesus as coming down from Heaven to the Mount of Olives. This will take place at the very moment the war of Armageddon reaches its final phase. The armies of Antichrist will be rampaging through the city of Jerusalem. When our Lord's feet touch the earth, the mountain will split, great topographical changes will occur instantaneously, and the assembled armies will be supernaturally destroyed. The Lord Jesus described His glorious return as follows:

> Immediately after the tribulation of those days shall the sun be darkened, and the moon shall not give its light, and the stars shall fall from heaven, and the powers of the heavens shall be shaken.
>
> And then shall appear the sign of the Son of man in heaven; and then shall all the tribes of the earth mourn, and they shall see the Son of man coming in the clouds of heaven

> with power and great glory
> (Matthew 24:29,30).

Revelation 19:11-21 describes the Lord Jesus as riding upon a white horse, followed by the armies of Heaven. He will be wearing a robe with the inscription, "King of kings and Lord of lords," and He will bring swift judgment upon the wicked.

The return of the Lord Jesus to deliver Israel from their foes and to establish His rule over the earth will be sudden and dramatic. The wicked, who thought they could defy God, will be caught totally by surprise. All will sense the tension of the moment, for it will appear that the forces of evil are about to win the victory. But the dramatic return of Christ in His glory will finally settle the matter.

A TEARFUL RECEPTION

When the Lord Jesus appears, He will be greeted with weeping — both by frightened unbelievers and by converted Israelites. I feel that both groups are included in the two New Testament passages which speak of wailing at the return of Christ. The Lord Jesus said,

> And then shall appear the sign of the Son of man in heaven; and then shall all the tribes of the earth mourn
> (Matthew 24:30).

The apostle John said that both Jews and

Gentiles will weep when the exalted Son of God makes His sudden appearance. We read,

> Behold, He cometh with clouds, and every eye shall see Him, and they also who pierced Him; and all kindreds of the earth shall wail because of Him. Even so, Amen (Revelation 1:7).

The unsaved will mourn because they will finally realize that judgment and punishment are inevitable. They will abandon all hope of Satan's ultimate triumph.

But Israel will mourn for a completely different reason (see Zechariah 12:10, 11;13:1).

Many Bible students, believing that this is the mourning of repentance by Jews when they see the returning Messiah, say that this is Israel's national conversion. To support this idea, they quote the passage in Isaiah where the prophet speaks of the nation as being born "in one day" (Isaiah 66:8).

Although these Old Testament passages may be construed to have this meaning, I am convinced that this interpretation is not correct. The teaching that Israel's national conversion occurs at the moment of the Lord's return contradicts a crystal-clear statement by the apostle Peter (Acts 3:19). And it leaves unsolved a number of other serious problems. I therefore firmly hold that the Jews of Zechariah's prophecy, who wail at Christ's return, are people who repented and believed on Him during the great tribulation. They will weep for sorrow when they think of how long their nation rejected their true Messiah.

If you read Acts 3:17-26 carefully, you will see that Peter was telling the Jews that the return of Christ to bring about the "times of refreshing" is contingent upon their conversion. He was saying that when they as a nation repent and believe, Christ will come back to usher in the golden age of Old Testament prophecy. Note: Peter did *not* say that Christ would return to bring about Israel's national conversion. Instead, it was the other way around. When Israel turns to Christ, then He will come back in glory. The Greek text of Acts 3:17-26 and most English translations are clear enough to leave no room for doubt. Israel will repent *before* Christ returns. The Old Testament prophetic passages must be interpreted in the light of this positive New Testament teaching.

A number of other considerations militate against the idea that Israel will be converted at the moment of our Lord's glorious appearance. Why, for example, would *unconverted Jews* risk martyrdom by refusing to worship the image of the beast? Relatively few Israelis today are deeply religious. Most would not be violating any strong belief by giving token obedience to Antichrist's religious demands.

Additionally, we can be sure that the 144,000 sealed Jews pictured in Revelation 7:1-8 are already believers in Christ, and that they are proclaiming Him as Savior and Lord. And the two witnesses of Revelation 11 must be believers in Jesus Christ as the Messiah, for God has no other way of salvation. Jesus declared, "I am the way, the truth, and the life; no man cometh unto the Father, but by Me" (John 14:6). The apostle Peter, dragged before the Sanhedrin for trial, told His accusers that they had sinned in rejecting Christ, and added, "Neither is there salvation in any other; for there is no other name under heaven given among men, whereby we must be saved" (Acts 4:12).

God has no religious halfway houses — not even during the great tribulation. People will be called upon to choose between the Lord Jesus and Satan. All who accept Christ will be saved. Those believers who live through the great tribulation will welcome the Lord Jesus when He comes in power and glory. The Jews among them will weep because the sight of the Savior will remind them of the centuries through which their people have rejected Him. And not one word in all the biblical portrayals of Christ's return give even a hint that the people who rejected Him during the great tribulation will be given a last chance to change their minds at the moment of His appearing.

Although God will be using the judgments of the great tribulation to punish the Jews and all mankind for their unbelief and sin, He is primarily preparing the human race for the Messianic kingdom. Moreover, since Jerusalem will be its capital city and Israel its central nation, the conversion of the Jews is an essential element in this preparation.

My friend, Christ *will* return, and He will bring peace to mankind. He will come when Israel as a nation accepts Him as Savior and Messiah. Therefore, the Jews do indeed hold the key to world peace.

6.
Israel's Glory

The nation of Israel has a glorious heritage and a thrilling purpose. For about 1,000 years of her history she enjoyed special visible tokens of the Lord's presence. A pillar of cloud during the daytime and pillar of fire after dark protected the Jews when they crossed the Red Sea, and led them through the wilderness. It hovered over Mount Sinai when God gave Israel the law, and it was a vital element in the wilderness tabernacle and in the temple constructed by Solomon. This cloud was a sign of their unique calling as God's chosen people.

But this visible indication of the Lord's special presence did not keep the Israelites from sinning. In spite of this supernatural sign, they repeatedly disobeyed Him and gradually adopted the immoral practices of their wicked neighbors. All the while, the Lord was patient with His people. He chastened them repeatedly by military defeats, draught, and pestilence. He caused the united kingdom of David and Solomon to become weakened by allowing it to be divided under Rehoboam. He permitted the northern ten tribes to be subjugated by Assyria. He let the armies of Babylon make repeated forays into Judah to take choice citizens into exile. Through all these years, however, the pillar of cloud remained in Jerusalem. In fact, it did not depart until 590 B.C. The prophet Ezekiel was a captive in Babylon when God gave Him a vision of the glory cloud slowly, as if reluctantly, leaving the temple in Jerusalem (see Ezekiel 10:18,19; 11:22,23).

This symbol of God's glorious presence, often called the shekinah, did not reappear when Zerubbabel returned and restored the temple. Nor was it seen in the magnificent structure built by Herod the Great. And if anyone who visits Jerusalem today wants to see it, he will look for it in vain.

After the nation was taken into captivity, many Jewish families turned to Jehovah and began to worship Him in truth and sincerity. But the nation as a whole continued to be alienated from the Almighty. When the promised Messiah, the Lord Jesus, appeared among them, only a few believed on Him. Even His resurrection and the powerful witness of the apostles did not bring the Jews as a people to an acceptance of Christ.

Because of their unbelief, the Jews have endured severe affliction. From the time they went into captivity until the present, they have been hated and bitterly persecuted. Even today the Israelis are having a difficult time. In addition to serious economic problems, they are living under constant threat of attack by their Arab neighbors. Moreover, Jews currently living in communist countries continue to be persecuted, and the majority of those who want to emigrate to Israel are not permitted to do so.

Israel does not enjoy her unique glory as God's special nation today. But the Scriptures tell us that this unhappy condition will one day come to an end. Jerusalem is destined to become the most beautiful and respected city in all the world, and the glory cloud will again appear in a new temple there. The prophet Ezekiel, after describing this millennial temple and the gates of the restored city, declared that its new name will be *Yahweh-shammah*, "The Lord is there." The shekinah that departed about 590 B.C. will suddenly reappear and fill the new temple (see Ezekiel 43:1-5; Malachi 3:1).

In this chapter I'm going to point to Israel's final regathering, her new covenant, and her perfect King as the elements that will constitute her glory in the coming kingdom age. You see, the setting aside of Israel during our present era is only temporary. She will once again enjoy God's special favor, and her restoration will bring great spiritual and material blessings to all mankind.

HER FINAL REGATHERING

One of the first acts of the Lord Jesus when He comes back to rule will be to regather Jewish people from all over the world to their homeland. The extent of this return will be far greater than any that occurred in the past. Though a remnant went back to Palestine under Ezra and Nehemiah, and some 3 million are there now, a vast majority of Jews have always remained in dispersion. When Christ comes again, however, He will bring His restless people back to their beloved land in peace.

The Old Testament contains literally hundreds of passages that prophesy this final regathering. (See for example, Deuteronomy 30:4; Isaiah 11:15,16; 27:12,13; 35:5-10; 52:12; 60:4,9,10; 61:5; 66:20; Hosea 1:11; 11:10,11; Micah 2:12,13; 7:15.) The Lord Jesus Himself will supervise their return, evidently using both godly rulers throughout the world and His own supernatural power.

Jewish people who trust in Christ during the coming great tribulation will have repentant hearts as they make their way back to Palestine. Jeremiah portrayed representatives of all the tribes uniting and weeping as they "go, and seek the Lord, their God" (Jeremiah 50:4). Ezekiel declared, " . . . ye shall loathe yourselves in your own sight for all your evils that ye have committed" (Ezekiel 20:43). Yes, they will be a humble and contrite people as they return to their land to fulfill their destiny. And when they arrive, they will join in the mourning of the Israelis already there, as described in Zechariah 12:10-14.

Not all of the Jews will repent, however. Not even through the horrors of the great tribulation! Ezekiel, speaking for the Lord, wrote, "I will purge out from among you the rebels . . . ." Then he added, "I will bring them forth out of the country where they sojourn, and they shall not enter into the land of Israel; and ye shall know that I am the Lord" (Ezekiel 20:38).

It follows, therefore, that the restored nation of Israel will be made up of born-again people. All the Jews who enter the millennium will have already accepted the Lord Jesus Christ as Savior and Messiah. The unbelievers who survive the great tribulation will be eliminated in the purging judgments described in Ezekiel 20:37-44 and Matthew 25:31-46. The prophet Isaiah wrote, " ... he who is left in Zion, and he who remaineth in Jerusalem, shall be called holy, even everyone that is written among the living in Jerusalem" (Isaiah 4:3).

HER NEW COVENANT

A second blessed element in Israel's future glory will be her enjoyment of the new covenant—a covenant far better than the one made at the time of Moses. Jeremiah described it,

> After those days, saith the Lord, I will put My law in their inward parts, and write it in their hearts, and will be their God, and they shall be My people.
>
> And they shall teach no more every man his neighbor, and every man his brother, saying, Know the Lord; for they shall all know Me, from the least of them unto the greatest of them, saith the Lord; for I will forgive their iniquity, and I will remember their sin no more (Jeremiah 31:33,34).

Though this new covenant is in effect for the church today, in that we are saved by faith alone on the basis of the finished work of Jesus Christ, it will not be fully realized until the Israelites are a forgiven and regenerated people.

In addition to this spiritual renewal of the Israelites, the new covenant will bring about a wonderful transformation of our physical world. When it goes into effect, God will erase most of the results of the curse. He will cause springs to gush forth fresh water in mountains and deserts. He will send rainfall that is neither too heavy nor too light for the environment. He will make "the wilderness . . . blossom like the rose," and will bring about the growth of bountiful crops (see Isaiah 30:23; 35:1,2; 41:18; 55:12, 13; Ezekiel 34:26; 36:29,30; Joel 2:21-23; Amos 9:13,14). Even the nature of wild animals will be changed. In Isaiah 11 we see the wolf, the leopard, the kid, the calf, the young lion, and the fattened ox living together without harming one another, and they are so docile that a little child leads them. Then too, the prophet Hosea recorded this promise from the Lord:

> And in that day will I make a covenant for them with the beasts of the field, and with the fowls of the heavens, and with the creeping things of the ground; and I will break the bow and the sword and the battle out of the earth, and will make them to lie down safely (Hosea 2:18).

We can be sure that hurricanes, tornados, earthquakes, droughts, and floods will not bring hunger, devastation, suffering, and death to mankind during the millennial kingdom. Apparently the Lord is also going to bring about some far-reaching changes which involve the planets and stars. In Isaiah 30:26 we are told that the sun and moon will give much more light than they do now.

In short, the fulfillment of the new covenant of God with Israel will be the spiritual inner renewal of His people and the transformation of the natural world. What a tremendous combination!

HER PERFECT KING

The third element in Israel's golden age will be the enthronement of the world's first perfect king—none other than Jesus Christ Himself. The angel of the annunciation told Mary that God would give to her miraculously conceived Son "the throne of His father, David" (Luke 1:32). Although the Lord Jesus is now seated at the right hand of God, He hasn't bypassed this Messianic earthly throne. On the day of Pentecost, Peter told his Jewish hearers that Psalm 110, a prophetic passage they knew well, portrays the crucified and risen Messiah. It indicates that He will remain at the Father's right hand until His foes are brought into subjection by the establishment of His earthly kingdom (Acts 2:33-35).

The Lord Jesus in His glorified body will actually come to Jerusalem to administer this Messianic kingdom. I don't think this means He will live on earth 24 hours a day. His permanent home is Heaven. Most likely He will commute between His abode and His place of work, just as people living in suburbs do today.

Under His rule, the manufacture of combat instruments of warfare will end (Isaiah 2:4), the poor and oppressed will receive justice (Isaiah 11:1-5), and evildoers will be punished quickly and fairly (Psalm 2).

During this 1,000-year interlude of Israel's glory, Palestine will be of special delight to God, "a pleasant land, a beautiful heritage..." (Jeremiah 3:19) Jerusalem shall be called "a city of truth," and its inhabitants will sing about its strength and glory (Zechariah 8:3). Moreover, Israel will be the dominant nation of the entire world. The Jews will influence all mankind politically, morally, and spiritually. Peace and prosperity will extend throughout the earth. In Isaiah 19, we read that the citizens of Egypt and Assyria will worship the Lord, and Malachi declared that this acknowledgment of Jehovah would be worldwide.

> For from the rising of the sun even unto the going down of the same, My name shall be great among the nations, and in every place incense shall be offered unto My name, and a pure offering; for My name shall be great among the nations, saith the Lord of hosts (Malachi 1:11).

Grateful for peace, prosperity, and righteousness, people from every corner of the earth will make pilgrimages to Jerusalem. They will join converted Israel in worshiping God at the millennial temple (Isaiah 56:7; 60:3; 66:23; Micah 4:2; Zechariah 8:21; 14:16).

Yes, the Bible teaches that the Jews hold the key to world peace. As God's special people, they are destined to become the center of His glorious kingdom. Universal righteousness, peace, and prosperity will encompass the earth when Christ returns. And this great event will occur when Israel as a nation repents and openly confesses Him to be the Messiah.